"UNTITLED VERSES"
FOR WHITE EYES ONLY

INTRODUCTION

It is with and in support of reminding the world of the suffering and brutal dehumanizing treatment of the people of the Continent now known as Africa and their descendants that these verses are written.

It is sincerely hoped that by keeping alive their experiences, as well as the hopes of both those who were enslaved passed, as well as those presently entrapped by a system of rules, equal in weight and brutality to the past, will result in the revolutionary move by those oppressed, as well as, those involved in the oppression of the oppressed, to destroy this cruel system driven only by greed and the desire to establish and maintain a manufactured system as well as status of superiority of "A" man over "A" people.

The monster of greedy exploitation, disguised in what is perceived at all levels of our society as being democratic and democratic governism, must be made to cease, for if allowed to thrive, will continue to bring humanized carnage over the entire universe as we know it.

The message here, is for those who and that continue to deliberately keep these reins of oppression, transforming itself into Racism, around the throats of those who continually and historically have had their lives as free people completely dominated and destroyed by this brutal system, will contribute to their own brutal self-destruction. For brutality breeds brutality. Inflecting of deliberate pain will result in the growth of deliberate specialized hatred.

Anthony Tharpe

Chapter 1

Grabbed from my land,
Fulfilling the covert plans of white hands,
I am now crammed, to many,
Like grains of sand,
many Nubians, Different, coming from
different parts of my great ancestral Land.

Fear leaps from our stares as they, they
seem not to care, care about our fear, fear
used to steer us clear of understanding their
undisclosed cruel plan.

I was snatched from MY land. MY LAND.
I was snatched from MY BEAUTIFUL HOME,
MY Fruitful LAND.
MY HOMELAND.

Pregnant women,
Little girls,
CRYING BOYS,
Solemn men,
All chained, all shackled,
Trying to understand.

After all we showed them out friendly hands,
When they first came to this,
This, MY LAND.

I looked over there,
He stood to stare, smiling at my people's fear.
This man didn't care.

Was he aware?
Is he aware?
Of the PAIN,
OF THE MONUMENTAL HUMAN DRAIN.
Is he sane? Is he insane?
Is he a reincarnation of my brother Cain?

I looked over there,

I saw the fear in his stare, as he watched his
child, snatched.
Wrenched from his woman's arms,
Their cries, their soul wrenching cries,
MY GUT WRENCHING PAIN.

The cries of their children,
The cries of my children,
The cries of his children,
The cries of her children.
His pain,
My Pain,
Her Pain,

Minds racing, heart pounding,
head exploding, Neck choking, breath leaping,
knees weakening,
Orifices exploding.
Captives shackled, chorus in moaning.
No place for pride, no taste for shame.
His pain, was my pain, my pain was his,
Her Pain became my pain,
Our pain became their pain,
our collective pain became a collective
mental drain, As the terror burned bright in
our brains, his brain,
her brain,
My brain.

Helpless, and hopeless,
Hopeless, and helpless,
I stood, he stood, we stood,
collapsed, helpless, bearing
the screams of his woman,
bearing the screams of my woman,
Bearing the screams of our women,
Bearing the pain of her man.

Seeing her empty arms, frantic, hysteric,
the screeching screams of his
fluttering children,
the screeching screams of my

fluttering children,
the screeching screams of her
fluttering children,

And at the first try I, They, he, she,
we, could not understand, Why!
Second try I, They, he, she, we wondered why.
Third try I, They, he, she, we refused to accept
and understand, Why!
Fourth try I, They, he, she, we were
in denial of the oppressive stance, WHY!
Fifth try I, They, he, she, we cried, WHY!
Sixth try I, They, he, she, we refused to comply,
WHY! Seventh try Many choose rather to die, WHY!

Then it became clear,
Everyone in chains understood.
A corrupt, evil, greedy man, would, if he could,
 Would, Where he could, if allowed he would,
Inflect inhuman pain, for his selfish economic gain.
FOR HE COULD.
And only then everyone fully understood, WHY!
why it was,
why it is,
Why it is always,
Always necessary,
For Everyone to became one.
To stand as one, against evil hands, against their
evil plans.

Women screamed and women moaned,
Girls stood strong, amongst lustful, violating,
flesh grabbing hands.
Warmen, hung their heads in desolate shame,
Some for playing so to,
To easily make due, with selfish,
Greedy, economic gain,
In spite of the human drain, in spite of the
innocent brain.
All Now trapped, by the same chains of
friendly betrayal, by which
the oppressor, selfishly gain.

Chapter 2

Images of my past keep grabbing,
Reaching forth each time with increased gain,
They scream my name,
THEY SCREEM MY NAME.
Mobbing, mobbing, mobbing,
Sobbing images.

I make a conscious effort to suppress
all righteous thoughts OF THIS INVISIBLE FORCE,
THIS EVER GAINING FORCE,
This ever screaming force,
Streaming, steaming realities of my past,
Reaching, preaching, teaching contradictions of
my 21ˢᵗ century mind, unequipped,
unequipped, unprepared to face the manufactured
lying
language of this time.
Unequipped to handle the commissioned
Crimes against people of all kinds,
Crimes of this time, Crimes of my time,
Crimes against people of our time, Across all time.

My Past keeps grabbing at me,
the fear with each encounter intensifies,
Its energy grown stronger ,
The encounters grows longer,
All Encompassing, leaving no route to escape my
Deliberately elusive thoughts.

Like a ship suspended in space,
Like a ship suspended in time,
My options are few, but mine.
I must face, that which approaches.
That which grabs at me, that past,
This past, my present, for it is mine.

I must face this vision which keeps
Grabbing at my very soul.
It conjures fear, of life, a real scare,
I must stare at this vision,
Which keeps grabbing at me,

Only then will I overcome this pervasive,
drains on lives by the Bain nemesis,
this fear that has kept me stagnant here,
From year to year.

Entrapped I am forced to look back.
I must look back.

Look back. Look back. Look back, at what?
I must look back at my ancestors,
My ancestors struggle from there to here,
From year to year.
I now want to move from fear to care.

These images I have fought with conscious thought,
These images I have fought with subconscious care,
These images I have fought with deliberate fear,
In these images' abyss I must stare.
These images have now become a vision I no
longer fear,
These images have now become a vision I hold dear.
These images have now become absolutely crystal
clear.

Like me here, my ancestors too had many scares,
Theirs to share,
Many fears, Steered by covert hands,
Hands with diverse brutal plans,
Hands with plans devised to hold me motionless,
Motionless,
in space and time.
A plan devised by the secret hands of a perverted
Man.

A generational plan, well designed,
deliberate, manipulative, with elements of

intoxication to entrap and
Incarcerate generation to generation
Of the misnomered minority nations.
reaching across these many years,
reaching across many generations,
to entrap the entrapped,
in time and space,
from taking their rightful place,
Amongst the human races.
Images keep grabbing at me, helping me to find
wonderful, liberating
Secrets, secrets that lay hidden in the shadows of
my mind,
My destiny, My life, My time!
Secrets that have unlock the shackles of my time.

Chapter 3

The muscles of my entire body quivers.
The strain of the chains seem unbearable,
I shivered.
My mind jumped between light and dark.
I could not talk.
My throat grew desert dry.
And I cried.

I looked up,
There was no beautiful blue sky,
I looked to the east, where the deceased rest,
I looked to the west, they pretend to be happy at best,
I looked north, where many battles are fought,
I looked south, the suffering is getting even worse.
There was no magnificent blue green mountains or
sky.
There was no breeze rushing to cool my lush
savannah,
Or the trees.
And I cried.

I looked around, the darkness sliced through
my chest,

The strain from the chains sliced my
woman's breast,
I was afraid.
And I cried.

My body shivered, I boiled from the steam
In the ship's Extreme,
the white of my eyes gleamed,
My mind began to rip at its very seams.
My soul screamed.
And I cried.

The OUTCOME was clear,
I looked back,
I saw my wives' fearful stares,
I saw the outstretched arms of my children,
And I cried.

Daddy, Daddy, help me.
Daddy, Daddy, break free,
Daddy, Daddy, help me.
Help me, Help Me,
And I cried.

The images moved slowly in my thoughts,
The images moved slowly across my time,
The sounds grew louder in my mind,
Like the chain ripping through my wife's
breast, the images penetrated my flesh,
The pain grew intensely unbearable as I lay
breast bear on my chest,
On a wooden bed, shackle, is my only protective vest?
My destiny, I dread,
My veins busting in my head,
As I threw up the slop, that I could not in my
stomach drop.
And I cried.

I saw chains dragged strong around my
children's necks,
The shackles around mine grew tighter and colder.
I felt helpless, I felt hopeless, I felt older.

The strain made a strong man weak,
And I cried.

Tears burned my eyes,
I could hear my children's cries,
I felt their fear,
The mist grew thicker,
The stench grew RICHER,
The stench grew RIPER,
The mist grew colder, I grew colder,
All thoughts rush my mind.
I could no longer hold her.
And I cried.

I looked to my left,
I Looked to my right,
There he stood,
He who came from somewhere far, far,
from here,
Distorted representations of Man, holding,
pulling,
smiling at my pain, for his selfish criminal
gain.
And I cried.

I looked ahead,
The door to my world became, a torture
in my head,
like thundering shutters collapsing,
the sound repeatedly, repeatedly, repeatedly
erupted AND MADE ME its captive.
I could hear the echoes of the corrupted.
His laughter grew louder, his laughter grew,
Louder, it grew longer, in my head,
His laughter grew stronger,
And as his language grew Fouler and Fouler,
And the waters grew deeper and deeper,
My children's screams became quieter and
quieter,
My children voices became a silent distant
whisper,
Soon I could hear them no more.

And I cry!

The Cries of my wife, became screams
in my head.
The PAINS of my children became that
of a spear
Lodged in my soul.
I could hold them no more!
I could see them no more, not as before!
And I cried.

My eyes closed,
My pain grew numb,
My mind became my world.
The door to my world, became as a torture
in my head,
I long for my wife's bed.
And I cried.

I still cry.
I closed my eyes, It closed the door to his
world,
I closed my door, it became as a torture in
my head.
And I cried.
I still cry.

Chapter 4

The world was a happy place, as strangers,
Strangely dressed men, our forefathers had
Mentioned landed, landed on our shores,
adding to life's excitement, in
Our green, green, land.

The word spared wide, the word spread far,
The natural hospitality of the people extended
themselves.
My people treated them, like rock stars.

There was consuming music as the
Nubian nation danced to the
Thump of powerful drums of
an excited nation,
Welcoming these evil humans
to this Nubian homeland.

Antelopes were plentiful across this
golden land before
It came into contact with this evil hand.

Suspicious my fathers were not.
There was no notion of their devious plot,
Such an evil plan, from a dubious MAN,
to drain my
People from their own land.

Bearing GIFTS, to create rifts,
between friends and neighbors,
FRIENDS ARE snatched, KIDNAPPED, TAKEN,
to their far, far, far away foreign lands.

There was no fear, when they first came here,
Many ancestors had long traveled there,
far across the sea,
For many, many, a year.

Their Plans forged by evil hands grew crystal
clear, Forcing the diverse Nubian nation to
THEM fear.

Then COMETH many more foreign Man,
upon MY LANDS, using their CRAFTED Plans,
to corrupt many Nubian Hands.
Corrupting plans, manufactured, causing
disruptive conflicts across My Nubian land,

Africans with generationally, easily corruptible
hands,
buying into this foreign man's evil plan,
Betrayals, confrontations, abductions,
Bringing many wars between the

Nubian Nations,
With alien arms, the hidden, purchased
Nubian hands,
This foreign man, waged war that
travelled afar,
Taking booty ,
Taking mothers,
Taking sisters,
Taking fathers,
Taking grandfathers,
Taking grandmothers,
Taking wives,
Taking husbands,
Taking sons,
Taking daughters,
Taking nieces,
Taking nephews,
Taking, babies,
Taking teachers,
Taking doctors,
Taking scientists,
Taking KINGS,
TAKING QUEESN,
TAKING PRINCES,
TAKING PRINCESSES,
TAKING CHIEFS
TAKING CHIEFTESSES,
TAKING PREACHERS,
TAKING HISTORIANS,
TAKING CULTURE,
TAKING HISTROY,
TAKING MEDICNE,
TAKING SCIENCE,
TAKING NUBINA.
TAKING NUBIA'S MUSIC,
TAKING NUBIA'S DISCOVERIES,
TAKING A PEOPLE'S COLLECTIVE KNOWLEDGE,
TAKING WORRIORS,
TAKING THE TEACHERS,

TO THEIR WAITING SHIPS,
SHIPS WITH THEIR HUNGRY BELLIES TO FILL,

With the spoils of a nation,
To be filled with the pride of Many
Nubian nations,
To be filled with the Heart of a
weeping nations,
To be filled with the BRAIN of a scared
Nubian Nation.

There was GRAVE resistance, to this
dehumanizing pain,
Many Nubians refused to be used,
Refused to be abused,
Breaking free, to find refuge in
the deep dark cold blue green sea,
Breaking free for Nubians to see,
Nubia is free,
Free to see that Nubia, has set in motion,
A resistance which crippled the brutal
acts of, This invading greedy, bloody,
feeling less, heartless MEN
FROM, a white nation.
Men Who have corrupted many, unthinking
nations,
Disrupting God's divine creation.
Still, this ILL with their bellies to be filled,
With the spoils of many a nations,
Corrupting hands of a man,
A man who continues to justify,
his genocide,
Of my Nubian Nation.
His evil hand continues to fill his holds,
with the Pride of many, many,
captive nations.

Chapter 5

I roamed my lush green land,
Having no development plan,
I was happy in my lush lush land.

My breast lay bare,

As I chased antelopes that looked
like deer,
I ran with lions with no fear.
I had little care, since my destiny
was Godly clear.
For like my ancestors before me,
For like my ancestors before them,
For like my ancestors before them,
And for them before them,
I was king in my land.
I was king, made by Gods Hand,
I was in my land, a gift from Gods
Creation,
To my Nubian Nation,
I was king in this, God's Creation.
Taking only what I needed, as was
the plan,
In God's divine Creation.

My Children laughed,
My wife smiled with passionate pride
and pleasure,
After all this was simply a part of our
natural care.
There was little fear,
Allowing us many, many, moments,
to show loving care.

My mind was never so pure,
My mind was never so clear,
My ancestors achievements was visibly
there,
My oral history was held dear,
My children grew in enlightenment,
I watched, my responsibility absolutely
clear,
from year to year,
My children were very dear.

Then came the scare,
A distinctly foul smell,
A foul smell that was strange here,

A smell that lingered, penetrating
the warm African Air.
Many pretending not to care,
Until for those in their loving cared,
were taken in the foul air,
Trapped, packaged, shackled like
common ware,
Family sold as chattel,
Handled worst then cattle,
then sold to strange smelling men
who were not from here.

This strange, man, came to this my
land to implement this,
This his cruel premeditated enslaving
plan.
Genocide, genocide, genocide,
Genocide spread wide.
The African population stupendously
dived.
In a way Never foretold, before, this
European arrived,
sold us like lamb chops on a block.
21st century genocide, his acts still
alive,
Without limit, it strives, crippling
unthinking lives,
Of Africans, of husbands, of children,
of wives.
With will, we stay alive, against all odds,
we grow and survive.

We overcome with will,
This genocide, designed to stop us
from being One,
That genocideic plan calculated to
stop us taking back our land,
from forging a united common plan,
on which to take a stand,
A plan that will protect each and every
one, every Nubian, every African,
every injured man, regardless of

where on planet earth he stands,
Or comes from.
PROTECTING EVEN YOU, Mr. WHITEMAN!
We are one.

Chapter 6

Standing on our own,
There will be no place to happily roam,
There will be no placed to peacefully
call home,
There will be no place to happily hold,
your wife, your child,
Even for the shortest while, so to shower
them with positive hope,
Love and joy.
Forget shellfish own, get grown, together
we can OVER COME what's left of vestiges
of those dedicated to
The Ancient and to ROME.

Chapter 7

I am caught in an ocean of hopeless loneliness.
A world of made up loveliness,
A world of built up bigoted lies,
A world with No one to love,
A world with No one to hold.
A world I have been branded to be hated,
I have been made to be feared,
I have been made to fear.

A world in which my life is filled with despair.
I have been Tabled, Labelled, fabled
By those who have declared,
Whites beware,
Stay clear, of the BLACK MAN,
The African Nubian, he has an angry hand,
United Europe must stand,

to effect the long standing
Genocideic plan, to reduce his numbers
across all lands,
Including his lands,
forcefully TOOK, from the African.

Chapter 8

From the ignorant, Mr. Whiteman,
Comes the angry white hand,
legally wielding weapons
of death upon African Land,
Across Nubia's golden
untamed sands.
Deliberately employed, they
are used to hunt the young,
To hunt the Young , the honest
innocent, Mr. Blackman.
To hurt all African, Mr. Blackman,
To Hunt the African, Mr. Whiteman,
United, Preached as one,
against them, All Europe must stand.
For Mr. Blackman, Mr. Whitehand
has made this, a harsh,
Harsh, life on this Africa's own land.

This is the foundation on which white
policy stands.
Policy contrived around a dubious plan,
to entrap the
Unthinking Blackman and those who
continue to pretend,
There is no such plan, even when it is
clearly visible in rhetoric,
In political pronouncements and Practice that
Go hand in hand, actively across this land.

Chapter 9

Black bodies, climb high,
Bodies Piled towards the sky,
Bodies hiding in the shadows,
hoping to get by,
As the racist man continue to
use their weapons,
Employed to covert man, employed
by covert hands,
To murderously shoot, another
human, another man,
Just for being an African,
A Nubian, an American Black Man.
Crying,
Pointing their lying hands at the
unthinking,
The deliberately blind,
The deliberately ignorant,
The deliberate Closet racist,
Being vindicated,
On the grounds that, this black man,
 raised his open, empty hands.
Vindicated on the ground that this
Blackman, had the nerve
To speak aloud that he is JUST a man.
To seek like all man, he too,
has a right to take a stand,
Even when he is stopped by one,
Who could be, a White Policeman.

Chapter 10

I am entrapped in a game of life,
I am entrapped in a game of hope,
I am entrapped in a game of destiny,
I am entrapped in a game of cruelty,
I am entrapped by a system designed
by a racist's man.
I am entrapped by a system designed

by judicious racist's hand,
I am entrapped by a system designed
to support racists prejudice,
I am entrapped by a system designed
to resist racial justice.
Justice for one, justice for everyone,
justice for every man.
I am entrapped by a system designed,
to hold power for only the Mr. Whiteman.
I am entrapped by a system, against
which it is RIGHT to stand.

I am caught in a game filed with lustful
cruelty, of unjustifiable hate,
Of biased prejudice, a game of
unthinkable, predetermined fate,
Lurking around every deliberately
constructed corner,
A game of life,
A game of hope, a game of destiny,
A game of death,
A game of unequal balance of life,
and of death,
A game founded in feeling less
hands of the foundation
Racist, Mr. Whiteman,
A man who pleasured, A man who
Pleasures in bleeding black hearts,
Erupting its syrup, leading to eventual
death.

Chapter 11

He cracked his whip,
Rendering my spirit weak,

The pain penetrating my soul.
The bruises on my ebony skin became
tinted with crimson,
as blood gushed from my chest,
my cheeks, my back,

I looked up, reaching out,
Hoping that my God would wrench
me from this pain,
This wretched pain.

This evil I had first welcomed
on my own,
this evil I had welcomed to my
own shore,
This evil, with whom I slept,
whilst I slept,
Silently he crept,
Pounced on me,
To Beat me, near to death.
This evil Beat me, mercilessly,
trying to break my will,
to take my tired breath.

It was sudden, then, I really felt,
I could really kill,
But still,
I held back,
Hoping,
Praying,
Praying,
Hoping,
That there might be some good in
this evil hand.
This seemingly evil man,
Hoping he may see my pain,
Hoping he could see my woman's
grief, feel my children's fear,
Hoping he could understand
why I bleed.

Instead, HE only, I MEAN, he only
 stared,
Looking remorselessly in my eyes,
I looked into his,
In his hidden SHAME,
He struck me. Stuck me again,

and again.

I really wish he knew my pain,
I really wished he knew my peoples
pain,
I really wish he knew, that someday
his children will feel my children's fear,
That his children will feel my woman's
pain,
That his children will have nightmares
of my children,
That his children will see Him,
inflicting on me,
Causing my crimson blood to
stain my life,
To stain my children's lives,
to stain his life.
That one BIG DAY, the world will
have to deal
with my nations drain.

That one day his wife will mourn
her violation.
That his soul will seek to hide from,
God's imposed reparation of his soul,
to liberate me,
To repay me for my suffering,
forced labor, my excruciating
Pain.
To repay for the,
The trapped suffering Souls, of my
dismantled Nubian nations.

Chapter 12

He covered up, using his arms,
But together we rushed,
His brother made, made good his
escape in the brush,

We caught one!
He tried to run,
With a flying kick, his body skipped
 over land,
Over asphalt, over roads, over green
fields of cane,
And Fields of Cotton groves.
Landing hard against the bricks,
Then falling on flowering vines,
climbing, the house of white,
It was clear,
The fall broke his hip, for
as he ran, he slipped.
With a punch on his lips, then
resorting to sticks,
We beat him savagely with willow
whips as he curled
Like a baby against cold,
white bricks.

With each blow he went low,
Then it was blow after blow,
He had no resistance to show.

His blood flowed.
And as if in the final act of a show,
I gave him a final blow.

He did everything to evade death,
And as if everything we had done,
was not enough,
I plunged my knife through his chest.
He struggled to find a breath.

As he grasped for his breath, while
gripping his wet vest,
he raised his head,
Reached up, as though struggling
to say, that's enough,

Desperate, he grasped for breath,
I looked down as his body became

outstretched, as
Though trying to rest,

His chest was wet,
The ground, his black blood met,
The dark ground made brown,
as red blood flowed from his
Neck, his chest, his breast.

Looking at the sky, he caught
my eye, And in a gentle pleading cry,
he begged, Why?

I pretended his quest had no effect.
This was nothing, but a killing fest,
And as His, WHY,
ripped through mine,
As he ripped open my lie, with a knife,
I made him
Finally quietly lye.
With not even a flinch, I reached for
his jugular,
mercilessly putting him to rest.

His why?
Imprisoned me and only then did his
powerful world
Take effect.
I never gave it much thought until then,
And like a burning arrow from an
invisible bow,
His words was as a powerful blow,
And my soul, still burns.

I executed a lie, just to impress,
Now I slowly die, for living a lie.
A LIE that caused so many to innocently
die,
While others become imprisoned,
A lie ignored, amidst the powerful,
profound word,
WHY?

Chapter 13

Into the holds of wooden ships
they drove us.
Stacked upon shelves, he packed
us tight,
like produce in a market place.
With not enough space,
Men, women, boys, girls, lay face
to face, a cramping fate,
contributing to the genocide,
a horrific disgrace.

Then the shutter slam shut,
Slowly eyes took to adjust,
Didn't matter much, for still,
the hold was darker than dusk.
And after centuries and decades,
this man still
acts as though his actions were just.
Some say what's the fuss;
the money empowered the, US.

For many a day, the ship
travelled far, far, away,
It rode huge waves, for days and days,
many captives went to the grave.
Men, women, children, boys, girls
all standing, all slipping,
All sliding, in this hold, of human
spoils and body waste,
sticking to form body past, bittering
to food and to the taste.

Stomachs emitted smells with each
ocean swell,
As men, women, boy, girls, like dead
flies, they fell.
The moans grew louder and louder
as we travelled further and further,

And Mr. Whiteman heard-ed her.
Mr. Blackman moaned her,
bawling bloody murder, to her herder.

Women screamed as white hands
fondled virgin breast
and cold dead flesh rubbed against
her smooth flesh as she laid flat atop
Shelves without any dress, riding
waves of death, the living hell.
For her unknown fear, to come, forced
wedding bell.
And the wooden ships continued to
sail west, this was at best a bloody mess,
As we travelled , bound, from east to west.
Death celebrated its fest.

Nubians all chained, chained the same,
Nubians chained in shame,
as white men perfected their money game.
 White Men made their daily count,
they totaled their Money to claim.
Absolutely No shame, even though
many were maimed.
Captives, dark, light, jet black or brown,
and many among, did drowned.
All treated the very same, as they
stand in squalor flowing across the ground.
Alive or dead, the black man gave no sound,
except to scream, groan and
Moan, with cries, for those who lay as
dead as stone, Lying on the filthy ground
And all places around, and around.
And Europe still lies, no shame, to hide
their gain.

Nubians all chained the same, in ships,
in shame,
Around and round, on shelve and on
the ground,
Sleeping and weeping, weeping and
sleeping

as the growls of their knotted guts,
would, Sudden erupt, for not eating
enough of the distasteful stuff.

And as the journey became longer
and longer,
and the Whiteman's coffers grew
fatter and fatter, stronger and stronger,
to the Blackman, his laughter didn't
matter, nor did the journey
which seem to be longer and longer.

Chapter 14

They shouted, They yelled,
These strangers, pushed, dragged, forced
and dragged us,
With much fuss, they pushed us to the deck
 atop, the dungeonous hold.
Liberated for a spell, our lungs swelled,
As the pungent smells leaped from our
chests while with buckets,
we were made wet, lightly cleansing our
pasty flesh, of hardened human mess.
And this ship continued to sail west.
This was a strange man at best,

Sharks were heard to rip the flesh, of
those who leapt or were thrown from
The deck. After all no money could
they make, for insurance sake,
they did not take.
These act kept many of us awake.
For if to slip, a captive would be made
sick,
But be fit, for insurance written slip,
 the Whiteman did Apply his whip.

Chapter 15

The sounds of gulls echoed deep inside
our holds,
The spirits of the enslaved leaped both
with anticipation and fear.
Adding to further scare.
The holds opened up,
Again we were placed on top,
The Net, gain, hung all around.
We searched, trying to find a way,
If not today, there will be another day,

Our cagers seem excited.
Looking, shouting.
As if saying, we'll be rid of you today,
They pointed our heads towards the dense,
White clouds,
Towering over a lush blue green land.
It reminded me of my Nubian homeland.

My thoughts rushed back to the others,
Others whose bodies would never be found,
In a brown ocean, where so many had drowned.
Cold sweat met my regret, it met my rage, it cooled
As it kissed my Flesh.

I never knew there was to come,
many more, tribulations to bear,
Yes, there was still much more,
in history to bear,
Fragile bodies, shivered under
the weight of bucketed water,
For a quick second I could swear
I saw my littlest daughter,
I imagined her happy laughter.

In their rush to wash us,
They fondled and touched us.
In jeering fun, they humiliated our men,
While shaming our women.
She looked away from us,

Her shame , became my pain,
And it burned bright, deep in my soul.

The weight of my violation brought
back memories,
Memories of my wife's vile penetration,
I remembered my sacred mother's
subjugation,
I remembered my father's humiliation,
And in frustration, my spirit shuddered
and shook.

Chapter 16

I killed a man,
Helped to destroy a nation,
To this day I cannot say why.
I remembered he try to ask me why?
Why he had to die.
I dare not lie, for I have,
 no valid alibi upon which to rely.

Absolutely no ground, or established
bound,
Other than the handed down desires
of my parents,
Of my ancestors, Hate, becoming my
welcoming hell's gate.
Ancestors who forcibly took them
from their homeland,
Their own land, for only being
a Blackman.

Chapter 17

I am angry,
I am guilty,
I wash, but my still I feel filthy,

And my thoughts of anger, my thoughts
of guilt, flows
Uninterrupted through my mind, my body,
my soul.

I constantly search for a reason,
I have found none.
Why did this man have to die?
Why did I support this lie.
And now the thoughts of guilt,
the thoughts of anger,
Flow through my mind.

For a living lie, an innocent
man had to die,
Why did I support this, living lie?
Blinded by endowed ignorance
and hate, a murder, I did make.
When will the prejudice dissipate,
When will my people become awake.
For peace sake, when will justice,
them make.

No longer will I live this lie.
No longer will I foster another to die.
My anger now makes me cry,
and each day,
Further I die,
Because I blindly, lived a lie and
caused another to die,
Robbing him of life's gigantic
delicious pie.

If you hate a man, make sure you
have a dammed good reason,
Why?
No one has to die, for a living,
inherited WHITE lie.

Chapter 18

Washing, scrubbing, shaving,
We wondered what was their craving.

They checked our teeth,
They oiled our skin,
They dressed some of us in strange
fitting clothes,
And used tightly fitting skins to rap
our toes.
I wondered, what were those?

From deep within, I wondered amidst
 the howling
Of the wind, did I sin or did I die?
Was there such a thing, as a collective sin?
The thought rode me, from the east
to the west Indies.
What justifying reason could I spin.

The strong,
The pregnant,
The children,
All packed, all stacked, in small boats
alongside chicken, herds of cows,
and even goats.
To each of us, New names,
our captives wrote.
The bitter sound, screamed
from their throats.

The bodies of the weak, the sick and
the dead, on ocean swells
they spread, they are swept.
All along our journey, our captive
often wrote their names,
in their journal's they kept, over
the deck they penned,
that many fell to death, on ocean
swells.

The living, who fell,
caused a cold ocean to be warmed,
burning to red,
As their bodies became fodder for
the greedy feeding frenzy.
For many, they became the envy.

Our braves, enriched, celebrating ,
what We would dread.
Many built extravagant, real estate
that spread from east to west,
Estates which complemented their
European mahogany desk.

What could I have done? To fall prey
to this inhuman?
What could I have done to feel the
hand of this brutal,
Unthinking evil man

Chapter 19

Do you know you have a hand in all the
problems across this
Planet and this, God's land, Man?!
You have, and continue to contribute
to the cruelty of man to man, by not
Taking a strong stand,
By not taking your stand, you allow
the racist to covertly band.

Indeed, very often you understand
much more than the average man,
Who are used to effect this evil lie,
Not just on man to man , but on Gods
divine land.
Even hurting, this very same, ignorant
unthinking racist man.

You have the wit,

You have the will,
Yet still, your silence, allow the
innocent blood to spill.

Being human,
Holding hand in hand, in spite of
the other color of another man,
Will fix, not trick, man to believe
racism no longer exist.
Let's for this instance be honest,
about the forced displaced
Race.
This gain, will provide added
solution to this problem, not
Provide volatile ammunition.

In deed man can walk hand in
hand as humans,
Not Blackman, not Whiteman,
not yellow man, not woman.
Let's all walk together across
this beautiful land.
Take a strong stand, let's
together rid ourselves of this color ban,
It's full time, we free the Blackman,
We really don't need a magic wand,
just honest humans.

This is a manmade problem,
deliberately spread across, God's gracious
Given land.
After all, Hate is Education passed
down from generation to generation,
From man to man.

Chapter 20

I refuse to hide my message behind
nicely written lines.
Yes I refuse to continue to educate,
through colorful words,
And nicely decorated white lies.

There is no time to continue to
disguise my journey across generations,
Yours or mine,
Its full time, we end this premeditated
crime, which has stretched long and hard
Across generations and time.

I need to reach you,
I need to teach you, so you get real,
Expose your thoughts against which,
from then
Till now, I still fight to be allowed
to appeal.
My fate is not sealed.

You need to understand my Pain,
my peoples drain,
It's a miracle we still remain sane.
I need you to see me for who I am,
For I will free me, so you will see you,
for what you are.
I want to free you, to make you see me,
for how I see YOU,
YES FREE YOU, NOT FOR WHAT you
believe I want you to be,
And certainly not so that you can
selfishly serve me.

Chapter 21

I helped you to survive, when I willingly
pumped my blood through
Your veins.
I taught the world how to fight the
elements, and how to build unexplained
Magnificent strictures, which have
survived the test of time.
I enlightened you to civilized rule.
I exposed you to healthy living,
I taught you about how to navigate
the stars, and how my ancestors
Travelled here from afar,
I taught you about medicine in Plants,
I brought sweet music to your
 desolate ears,
I liberated you in dance.
I extended my hand, when
you needed a friend
I held your hand, when you were blind,
I taught you of the comfort of
religions, stretched across magnificent time,
I showed you the value of the harmony
 between nature, God, man and time.
I charted the path from the eastern
sands to western lands,
so you could find me, to save you.
I even told you that one day, man will walk,
woman and man,
together on celestial lands,
Most importantly I taught you the
significance of the essence of life, of God,
of man.
I had such wonderful plans when
we first shook hands,
Instead you defied me, made contemptuous
covert plans with a greedy ONE,
TO KIDNAP me, to sell me, TO incarcerate me,
for profit to gain off me.

I just can't understand?
Where did I go wrong?
Why did I deserve this cruel betrayal
of my friendly Hand?
When all I wanted to do was to
enlighten you, to emulate
the good of the other, not to destroy
each other, my brother man.

Chapter 22

Remember, whatever you force me to be,
will without a doubt, one day affect,
You, me, WE!.

Chapter 23

I have tried to understand my fate.
It is not without deep trenches of
contradiction that I through my faith
have deliberately and desperately
tried to justify my fate.

The answer to my questions
eludes me, like a fox eludes his hunters.

I have knelt with tear filled eyes,
Reaching up in my white painted
prison of earthly existence,
Hoping that God will reach down,
take my hand, liberate my soul, with
help to enlighten you and rescue me,
from the hands of my racist brother's
stand.

I have confused apprehensions about
my fate from birth to my very passing,

The hate of another man,
The beauty of my ancestral homeland,
God's plans consumed my every thought.
I face a fate, which has left me exposed
to the brutal abuse of another man,
Yet I know, I am in Gods hand.

This mystery of the illusive harmony
of the things of nature and man
Absolutely astonishes me.
One day soon, the answer to my
questions will free me, free you, free we.
Free me to liberate me, from a blind faith,
from those who selfishly hate,
for economic gain.
I face the contradiction in a divine creation,
Designed with efficiency and
endless heavenly constellations,
which has evolved a brother,
whose confused envy and jealous hate, drives
our defined fate.

Chapter 24

I thank the lord of the havens, the lord
of the four winds,
The lord of the sun,
The lord of the moon,
The lord of the stars,
The lord of the cool dark, deep oceans,
The lord of my ancestors.
For I have been blessed.

Yes I have been blessed, with the
ignorance of not knowing,
Knowing how to hate or participate
in hate as a privilege of place.

I refuse to make an enemy of my
white brother or any other,
Black , white, yellow brown, all are
equal in my mind and the
Periphery of my soul.
I have been blessed , for I can find
no legitimate reason to hate an
Entire race.
I have been blessed, for I can
recognize the difference between good
and evil, between light and ignorance,
between the beauty of life and the
desolation of hate.
I understand the difference between
everlasting life and the dark
Ravines of absolute damnation and
death,
Death, the desired chosen course
of racist nations.

Chapter 25

The strength of one individual reflects
the strength of the
Entire nation.
To truly destroy another, we must
destroy his ability to live , his ability to love.
The continued promotion of engineered
endowed distrust and hate,
will effectively achieve the total destruction
of a man exposed.
The destruction of this one man will
spread to another, eventually leading
To the destruction of the entire nation,
The destruction of the universe.

Chapter 26

I've seen many broken men, made into mere tools,
for another mortal man.
Committing acts impressed by those they
choose to follow.
Men when left alone to reflect finds little pleasure
In the acts done to impress the other.
Men who find hard lumps in what used to be
comfortable beds.
Men who now taste only the bitterness of lies,
lived in the shadows.
Men who seek refuge from their conscience,
where there is none.
Now you tell me man,
Those of you who choose to blindly follow
another,
Why Brother, would you choose to
knowingly wrongly follow
Another, who obviously isn't your
brother and blindly join him
To kill your brother?.

Chapter 27

I likened my history to that of a church mouse.
I move and do as I must as the world sleeps.

Out of sight out of mind, living off the nation's dime,
That used to suit my lifestyle just fine,

Until one day a stranger, one that I have never
seen before,
Came knocking at my door.

I opened it and welcomed him in.
While I fed him, his eyes roamed all around,
around my kingdom,

my castle, my life.
Like a starving eagle, silently, swiftly,
he struck.
No longer am I king of my castle.

Being critical of my ways, he brutally
forced me to comply to his,
He worked me, in many ways, over many
long days.
CHANGING MY LIFE, MY KINGDOM,
MY Kindred, in brutish
Horrific ways.

Sometimes I'd close my eyes wishing
that this was nothing, but a
horrible nightmare,
I became painfully aware that
my fate is real,
It stirred widespread fear.
No longer was value of my life dear.
My oppressor had only one plan.
That was to ravage this
newly found land, my body.
Ignoring life, nature and me in
his greedy plan.

Chapter 28

I looked up,
The universe looked back, overpowering
my imposed
Thoughts of being king of my destiny.
I became like that of a microscopic
creature in an ocean of
diverse divine beauty.
No longer did my ego take precedence,
I shuddered in my bewilderment.
The peering, twinkling eyes of this
mother of creation.
This mother of all life.
The cool comforting beauty of her

deep dark, black void
Left me only in lustful ignorance.
Ignorance opening the door to the
universe.
Ignorance that open the door to
God's universe.
A universe which opened up,
enlightening the door to mine,
and creations all divine.

Chapter 29

It is easier to truly fall in love by
allowing our natural
Instincts to search and select rather
than an Educated resolved search.

Very often our entrenched ideas
leads to elude that which
Would have made us truly happy.
The religious belief that the future
 is planned.
The mystics rides on the belief
that his stealing glimpse
Of the future will assure destiny.
The truly pure man allows his
thoughts and heart
to appreciate and love the present.
The true love in us will come alive
if we seek beauty.
The truly conflicting act of creation,
the educated attempt to methodically
seek differences,
will lead to contempt, distrust
and hate.
A fate which will leave us in
competitive turmoil.
In beauty we find love,
In love we develop shared
unconditional understanding.

Chapter 30

Today I heard a Blackman with one white
glove on one hand
Scream, " It doesn't matter if you are
black or white",
In a mighty voice, he sang, he danced.
He spun with such fury, it was electrifying.
Like electricity, his words have been for
centuries life defying.
His word were lying.
Lying words, lying words, passed down
from one defiant generation to the other.

Isn't it time we truthfully say why the
Blackman are amongst the highest in
dying?
Isn't it time we stop this constant
deliberate lying.
Is it not that, it doesn't matter,
if you are black, but matters only
if you are white.
Isn't it time to teach the youth
the truth?
STOP THE LYING, REAL PEOPLE
ARE DYING! Stop the lying.
Only then will we rid ourselves of
the constant protests and crying.
Only then will we rid ourselves of
the nonstop dying.

It shouldn't matter if one is Black,
It shouldn't matter if one is white,
But for you AND me, those who rule,
rule only with white in sight,
Steadfast white might, driving
civilized me to fight, casting the
World into continuous night.
WOULDN'T it be just simply right
if we stopped this ongoing fight,

And truly liberate right, not continued
unequal white might.

Wake up all humans, of all races.
We need to face all the deliberate
falsities generating racial hate,
only then will we become human
enough to break this longstanding
spate in compromised waste.

Chapter 31

It is not easy to face the world each day,
knowing for no fault of Your own,
no fault of creation, you stir violent
human emotions
Of hate.
It becomes especially more difficult
when you realize how so many try to
impress their guilt on me, for the
figments of their own imagination,
as they Live in the world of denial
and manufactured ignorance.
Oh how I sometimes wish I could
turn back the hands of destiny and time,
then return to my wild, wild, natural
pure world and life, with life in sight.
My world, before exploitation, before
my forced migration,
before my forced flight.

Chapter 32

If you can educate, then you can spread
understanding, not hate.
If you can teach empathy, then you can encourage
the growth of
Compassion,
If you can preach love, then you will teach happiness.
If you can eliminate lust, then you will promote
passion.
IF YOU CAN eliminate greed, then you will destroy
brutality.
If you can teach the world to listed and understand
the music,
Then the universe will know how to dance.
When you teach the young all these things, then our
adults
Will be like children.
If you can grow children so exposed, the we will have
world peace.
When we achieve this, then we will have planetary
happiness.

Chapter 33

A brother is caught in a violent clash.

 A social catastrophic match brought on by the greed
Of men, that have a driving need to climb, climb by
Piling, piling UP, quarters and dimes, earned by the
sweat,
Yes, the sweat of my fathers, the labor of my mothers,
The violation of my sisters,
The blood of my brothers,
For hour on the hour, another brother, a black
brother, dies by a system being held in place by a
white power.

Look in this mirror my white brother, for this is

Written for white eyes only.
Death hour on the hour, for those
struggling to survive
In this system of white power.
Hanging on a corner from dusk to dawn,
dealing in
Flesh, dealing in white power,
A power causing Murder,
A power committing murder.

How much longer?
How much further can you sit back
and allow this?

Look in the mirror my white brother.
Remember Murder, hour on the hour
of a black brother,
By white power.
How much longer can you bear to stare
at a colored world
Through your white mirror?
Through your fabricated white eyes,
without grieving the
Injustice you have done?
Remember, murder hour on the hour
of your colored brother by a
System held in place by a brutal lying
white power.
Remember this is written for white
eyes only.

It's real, many don't have a choice,
they must deal, fighting hard to
Survive on the killing fields.
The white fields of COKE, The brown
fields of DOPE,
THE BLACK FIELDS OF HOPE.

That isn't the life they were born to live,
my white brother,
That's the life, forced upon them
by a system,, held in place

by a white power, causing murder
hour on the hour, brother
on brother, all in the name of white power.
Look in the mirror,
Look in your eyes,
Look in mine,
Search your thoughts,

Now you tell me, my white brother,
As the body count climbs hour on
the hour, in support of white
Power.
Who is really living a lie?
Look around, see what's going down,
Open your eyes my white brother,
We will all die in your painted world
of living lie.

Warm your hearts my white brother
Remember murder by a brother, by
a brother.
Murder by a brother by another,
brought on by a system
held in place by a white power.
White power,
A system you can quickly change
this hour.

How much more can you stand to hear?
How much more can you stand to hear?
How much more do you expect me to bear?
How much longer can you sit there
in your white
World thinking my life is fair.

Chapter 34

I've always been conscious of the ego or man.
I've always tried to understand this drive, this
desire to succeed.
I've even had the unyielding desire to compete.

I've seen the benefit of cooperation,
I've seen the joy of dialogue.
But in spite of all my human thoughts'
in spite of all my human
Interests
In spite of all my human intellect,
I've never seen the benefit of war.

A concept lucratively grown, by those
in disguise.
Out of sight,
Those Far from the killing fields.
War for profit, promoted with little care,
Little care, for life, for another's life,
for a bothers right.
Promoted for the fabric of economic
growth, and capital gain.

The true fabric and fiber of human
cooperation and therefore
Universal existence totally ignored.
War leaving only painful scars in nature
and of man.
War, leaving death, War leaving debts.
War in which only the instigator
becomes wet, totally saturated in
His selfishness,
In his ego,
In his economic gain.
A gain achievable at the expense of
humanities ultimate loss,
Your loss, my loss, our children's
collective loss.
Gains if unchecked, will consciously
consume the innocent,
The ignorant, the unaware.

Chapter 35

Can you hear the drums?
Vicious, violent beating drums.
Heavy drums.
Drums being beaten, by the thumps,
From me, Suite-Ala Bengee,
A man you call Nigger, A man whose
brother is murdered
By the squeeze of your trigger,
A man you call Nigger, whose sister
you Groped, my brother.
The man you call Nigger, only because
I seek to be free.
I seek to see.
Go figure?
Will you try to be me?
Only then will you see me;
Suite-Ala Bengee.
Then and only then will you
understand and see,
Why I must be free.

Why be me?
Why be Free?

Yes I.
I, must be free, me Suite-Ala Bengee,
Do you understand that, I
Suite-Ala Bengee, don't belong to thee!

Let this be a warning to thee, from me,
Suite-Ala Bengee.
I don't need you to make me free.
You must set me free from the shackles
of your mind, Not mine.
Free me from the prison of
your thoughts, or I will become
That which you have invented
of me, to keep me from being free,
Me Suite-Ala Bengee.

Free me from thee, or I will become
your Boogie-Man.
The nemesis of your nights, and
your heathen
In the nightmares of your day.
Do you wish to live that WAY?

Your nights will become my day
to play, I will justify this
New way to make you pay, unless
we build a new day,
Where I have a say in the way I
live each and every day,
That's not necessarily going to be
your way.
This is my mission. Don't even dare
to think I need your permission,
This can be easy, it's absolutely your
decision.
Will you intelligently and peacefully
adapt this position?

The position of me, Suite-Ala Bengee.

Yes Suite-Ala Bengee, will, if not, pay you
With havoc in your drams.
Yes me in your dreams, Suite-Ala Bengee.
For all I need you to do, is free me
from your shackled mind.
Yes, ALL I WANT TO BE, IS TO BE
 FREE OF THEE, free to BE ME,
Suite- Ala Bengee.

I can no longer tolerate your depressing
weight filled with
Human hate.
You have constructed a river of human
emotions, to deliberately
Spate, into the unnatural harrowing
motion of hate. Such a disgrace.
Your fatal mistake.

I Suite-Ala Bengee, Yes me. Can you see ME?
Yes ME.
I AM willing to extend a friendly handshake,
in an attempt,
To displace your unnatural, uncalled for,
unchallenged hate.

Then we'll become friends,
We'll become even playmates.
It's no greave impediment for you to,
Stop, wait, listen, even emulate,
before you continue this unnatural hate.
Let's fix the manmade, harrowing,
fate of me, Suite-Ala Bengee.

There is no need for me, or you, or
either of us to ego-ly
Be heavyweights.
I'm no longer willing to wait, or
tolerate your hate,
Of me, Suite-Ala Bengee.

You will not be allowed to maintain
Such an inhuman State,
It's now time to liberate your ignorant
mind and get to know
Who you claim to hate, me, yes me,
Suite-Ala Bengee.

You may choose to resist and hesitate
 prolonging a policy or hate.
You may arrogantly continue to generate
your system of hate.
But then watch me, me Suite-Ala Bengee,
inflate my suppression of
Your kind of hate,
I will oppress and compress your hate,
yes the hate you taught me,
Me Suite-Ala Bengee.

Let's jointly break this, your manmade

fate, of generated hate.
Let's instead build on the hope of
being friendly MATES,
Yes the friend of Suite- Ala Bengee,
a man you did nigger name,
A man willing to end hate. Let's
begin to live, celebrate, instead
Of facing off in a Desolate State.
Where, if unfixed, your well
taught hate, will
Naturally spate, to make a homeland
a barren, boring, uncultured place,
Filled with human waste, and of
manufactured educated hate.

My race, yes me, Suite-Ala Bengee,
has been GREAT to tolerate this
tremendous
Torturous hate,
Hate from a man, who take pleasure
in human degradation,
human HATE AND HUMAN WASTE.

Stop this hate!
Or watch me, yes me Suite-Ala Bengee,
quickly close your freedom gate.
Yes me, Suite-Ala Bengee,
An African Great.

Chapter 36

Yes I'm MAD!
Anger rages inside me with a heated rush.
I'm transformed from good to bad, making
every living creature
Beside me sad.

They say I'm bad.
They say the pressures of life has driven
me pass mad.

They say I have been made insane.
What a game.

I can see nothing but my pain.
I can feel nothing but my pain.
I can feel nothing but the piercing
spear of your suppressed hate.
It makes me MAD.
It makes me Sad.

Like Vesuvius, I often erupt.
It consumes what little love I have
to give, up.
I am frightened while being amazed,
at my deliberately suppressed rage.
It helps me, to continuously be,
on God's page.

My anger rages on.
In sudden natural reaction, my
 body leaps into tractions,
Bringing the monster, built, it comes
alive.
I am possessed with unnatural drive,
and destruction shortly arrives.

And my war rages on.
They claim they don't understand,
They claim I don't behave as a
righteous man.
They claim not to see, the hidden
jolly green giant that I am,
They refuse to see the connection
between, who they
Perceive me to be, and my desire
to be free.
They refuse to see, how I have been
deliberately maimed
By unclean hands, across many lands,
From Washington to
The crying African sands.
They refuse to take a stand, against

the demise of my people and
My exploited homeland, at their hands.

My pain forces the monster in me,
like an immortal,
Like a giant, to roar with trembling
emotion, driving
My mortal sole into violent,
unchecked chaotic commotion.

Looking around, almost alone,
my monster faces his own fear.
Alone and afraid, alone and in fear,
alone and in fear.
Like a war Drone after a mission,
empty, grey and alone.
Suffering from what murder
deliberately done.
My monster is cold as it hits the
 ground.
O how much, I miss the child within.
O how I wish I could awaken my
child within.

But I know, I cannot, I must continue
to protect him from
This racial sin, with Witt, from my anger within.
I am forced to live with my constructed
dam of frustration,
Anger, fear and heated volatile emotions.

Chapter 37

It seem you always claim, that your, faults,

are never yours, but always mine.
I say yes, you always say no.
I want to stop, you always force me to go.
I want to run, you always say, its best to go slow.
I try to walk by your side, you always try
to hide, for the sake of your pride.

I fight to liberate, you always fight to control.
I want to enlighten, you always fight to keep
me in the WHITE.
I fight for my rights, you make laws to
say I'm a rebel.
I try to comply, you always encourage me
to revolt.
I tell you the truth, you always hide behind
a lie.
I pray for wisdom, you always laugh and
call me a fool.
I finally get tired, I agreed with you,
You say I should think for myself.
I hide my face, you pull my hand.
I run from you, you always run faster
to keep up with me.
I break the cycle to be free, you say let
things be.
I guess one day God will let me see,
why you fight to hang-on to me.
Only then and only then will I be
truly free of thee.

Chapter 38

Their chains!
Their whips!
Their torture! failed to break my
quest for my freedom.
Each time they chop one limbs, I
 somehow grow another.
I run stronger, faster, further to
my farther.

They broke my bones on the wheel.
They chop my foot at my heel,
THEY TOOK MY NAME!
Then THEY branded me, "BUCK X" with
their scalding iron.
And even when they believed my body
would collapse,

They worked me, unnaturally, for free.
Yet I continue to soar above the
heavens for them to see.

I remembered my freedom,
I remembered being happy.
I remembered how to love,
I remembered my children,
I thought of my wife.
I look at your children daily,
born to my sister, my daughter,
my wife.
I looked daily at your sons and
your daughters,
Bourn by your daughters.
And I weep at this life. And
I weep along with my wife.

For profits made,
And for Fame gained, you sold
my children.
You sold your children,
You raped my wife.
And you maimed my life
Then claimed, this is your right.

Your children carried my wife's
blood in their veins.
Yet they all remained sane.
Passing so they would gain
The advantage to thrive,
Like Solomon, they were wise,
Like us before them they survived.
The oppressors fear, in
panic spate, created genocide, against
Your own child, numbers rising strong,
against YOU evil man, they rise,
You who grabbed me, from My homeland,
Now we are strong,
Now we will take our stand,
If you want to survive Mr. OPPRESSOR,
Man, remove

Your imprisoning chains.
Chains which you have used to
Brutally prevail over this diverse
colorful race.
No longer will we allow you to
carry out your hateful genocidal plan
Over this planet's man, Not on
 my land, you racist one.

Get my meaning man,
For like me, there are many
of you, many amongst you,
Who have come to see the wrong,
With me, they now stand, to
fight this racist plan.
No longer will separation,
No longer will the shade of
our hair, the shape of face or the shade
Of skin, stop us from being one,
stop us from standing strong, standing,
As One.
We all are equal according to God's
MASTER PLAN.
From meek, from humble, from oppression,
United we will justly rule this land.
You must know , it's time to give upon
your racist stand,
A failing plan. Implemented by your
devilish hands.

Chapter 39

On racks we became packed.

As they stacked. They felt, they rubbed,
they touched,
They groped and grabbed us in all our
private places.
Passed from one hand, to another man,
Families are again split.

Sent to many different places.
With many Different, they were forced
to share spaces.
Many humans, many Nubians, many
captive Africans,
Forced to work for white painted faces,
in big Agricultural places.

Hurting , sad faces,
Hurting, lost faces, in unknown distant
places,
Like common animals, they were
herded,
Counted as livestock, placed atop
public bidding Box.
Evil ones felt they had the right, to
take stock, of an entire race,
Compelled to work, forced to whore,
they are now
 wearing, sad, sad, faces.
Forcefully bread, in Cold cramped tiny
Spaces.
Men, women, selected and branded,
forced to breed
In open view, worst that a zoo.
Men became chameleon like stallions
and Bulls,
Bred to be rubbed and brushed to be studs.
Women branded breeders,
And the Whiteman forced them to be their
pleasers.
Other of us were made as field seeders,
and fear induced heeders.
Children grown like prize stock, sold,
on blocks, with profit gain
From their tiny backs.
For many this was a tremendous shock.

What could drive one man to sell
another man like life-stock?
In this new land, I was never
treated as a man.

This philosophy is part of deliberately
constructed plan
For one man to dominate Gods land,
God's first made MAN.

My woman was freely used and abused,
Then passed on to any Whiteman,
 this by the hand of the oppressor man.
Those who resisted were beaten,
killed and or shot, placed prominently
On high post atop the biggest hill tops.
Their blood freely spilt, it didn't take
much to justify, their kill.

Now you tell me Oppressor man,
isn't that putting up with a lot?
from Men who felt great when
they raped,
from men who had no regret,
when they discarded the products of their
Forceful violation,
of the man and woman of this captive
brutalized nation,
Acts which continue to create
much frustration.

Chapter 40

Hey! Hey! HEY!
You! Yes You,
How does it feel?
In fact do you know what it feels like to
stand by, shackled, beaten, groped
Fondled, then raped?
Can you conceive, what it is like to see,
see your wife,
Your daughter,
Your mother,
With ruined lives,
Trapped Under your oppressors

penetrating weight?
Can you? can You?
Can you bear to stare at them, ripped,
bleeding, hear them crying?
Can you understand why so many,
shamefully bawled unstoppingly to die,
Willingly taking their life?
Crying, ashamed and in pain,
when the CRIME,
THE guilt was not hers, but Yours!

Now you say why?
And you really sit there now,
pretending to be ignorant,
Asking why?
Why do me, them, us, we,
have a shared shame, enraged
for your inflicted
Violation?
then forced to live a compromising
lie in a denying Nation.
Belittling,
Belittled, in his woman's eyes,
Belittled in her lovers eye.
Belittled in his daughters eyes.
CAN YOU UNDERSTAND,
THE BLACKMAN'S PAIN?
CAN YOU UNDERSTAND WHY HE CRIE'S?
Can you understand why so many
Africans always cry?
Can you understand why so many
don't mind to die?

Can you imagine your woman,
your daughter, your mother being forced
To have the child of her violator?
To see her violator in her child's faces,
each and every day?
To be bred with another, like a horse,
a cow, a goat, in pungent stables?
Can you understand, why
"Bloody murder we wrote"!

And the pain still grows.

CAN YOU UNDERSTAND ME?
For if you do, then you will understand
why I could not reject, her child,
Reject your child, reject her.

My white brother, your acts are Vile!
You need to stop awhile.

Don't condemn me for raising your Black
white child,
I accepting them as mine, not punishing
them with guilty thoughts, of their Fathers
WILD, who continue to be vile to their own child.

Chapter 41

The dawn is kissed violently by the morn.
Her cool face rumpled by forked tongues
of lightening tips,
Ripping her.
Brightening dimness to her morning light.

Clouds filled, hunting for the time to deluge
Mother earth, washing away all the built
up anger, hate and rage.

The storm meets the morn.
This is the dawn of the dawn of storms,
The dawn of all storms,
The dawn of all dawns.

Like a grain of sand,
Like a grass strand, all human must stand,
against those with unclean hand.
They have angered the guardian of this land.

The fear is great, carrying much weight,
hidden in trembling emotions.
For many, giving rise to intense

combustible commotion of fear visible in
their stares.
With fear, boldly comes deep tears.

Like raindrops, turning into massive streams,
Flowing, bruising, scaring the face of the earth.
Scaring the Place of MAN. This blessed land.

Streams, move into rivers, rivers rush to
be oceans,
rushing with violent abrasion, as if
With a definite purpose to disturb God's Creation.
Working incessantly, knowing its limited
time to erase and remove
the layer of built up evil of human hate of
natural ingrate,
trying tediously to cleanse this sweet, sweet
land of the evil of man.

Like a mighty fan, the storm blows,
it moves along,
spreading violently, ripping
Many from this land with a punishing hand.

Many are wiped out of sight.
Many who we thought were right and
righteous.

O God where did we go wrong?
This day will give rise to many a sad song,
across this white
Really white, land.
The storm ripped many a man from the
bosom of the land.
All because man went along with a
corrupt system, a brutal plan,
Designed to distort righteous thoughts
of the rights of the Blackman.

Chapter 42

Can you imagine your world filled with pain
and grief.
I don't mean seeing someone else in pain.
I mean you feeling this pain.
A pain so intense, you often pray for absolute relief.
Can you imagine a pain so real, you beg for God's
total review,
For if you can.
Then I know you can understand mine.

Chapter 43

Casual observer what do you see?

As an active participant, how do you feel?
Do you understand the game of life?
Can you see the mistakes visible from the sideline.
CASUAL OBEREVER are our mistakes Obvious?
Are the corrections to you clear?
Are we as players consciously aware?
Or though we are involved do we remain unaware?

TO YOU THE CASUAL OBERVER, IS IT CLEAR?
To the players there is often hidden fear,
To you casual Observer is the game clear?
Casual Observer is this game fair?

If so, how long will you stand and just
observe this fear?
Is it that, it is not within you to care?
Is it for you, casual observer, an even
greater hidden fear,
To show publicly that you care?
Is your fear so great, you refuse to
help liberate those trapped
In this game of life and hope?
Casual observer are you enlightened enough,

to build a shared world
Of life and hope?

Chapter 44

It is hard to conceive of a universe totally
composed with men from all worlds and from
all dimensions, engrossed in absolute love,
in absolute caring for one, and all others,
in spite of looks, color, or creed.

It is hard to conceive of a universe totally
composed in dimensions of thought, defined
by our so called wise, of wisdom learnt.
Wisdom, Not of natural occurrence, but by
manipulated instructions.
Wisdom totally lacking, or lurking in the
shadows of the pure man's minds, or
Lurking in the minds of the consciously
subconscious, or even of the innocent.

The innocent who become molded in
ways profoundly of the wise,
Of ways which have transformed joy to pain,
Transform love to hate,
Transform ignorance to bigotry.
Wisdom that a truly conscious caring world
need not
Become aware, Of wisdom conflicting.
Wisdom we really do not need.
That wisdom of our egotistical intellect.

Chapter 45

You may come along, or you can stay and face
 my wrath!
No longer will I silently support the illusion of
your control over me,

And over mine, over my mind.

Because I've often chosen a path to remain silent,
And because I've chosen not to ravage your
bodies with brutality,
as you have done to mine, along with the brutality you
continue to unleash upon me, you really believe
you rule me.

You may choose to become enlightened,
Or you may choose to remain the condemned,
You may choose to be arrogant,
You may choose to remain the ignorant fool
You pretend to be, or you may choose to lets
be happy and free.

Chapter 46

I've been here before time began.
The time has now come when I will no longer
allow, you the prodigal
Son, to design plans to destroy God's first Son.
Consider this a final warning.
A profound notice for you to put your brutality
down,
or face this sticky web which you have spun,
my prodigal son.
There is a limit to your unchecked cruelty,
to me, God's first Son.
Your cruel game is getting hotter and hotter.
Together we can overcome, instead of having
a fatal face down.

Chapter 47

My History has been one of intense turmoil,
All the pain,
All the frustration,

All inhibitions set aside,
It has been a rich one.
My survival against all the odds has
shown my oppressors,
My nation's strength.
My unbroken will and resolve
determination has broken
His will, while strengthening mine.
Against me there have been many crimes.
Yes, I have had enough compassion to
reach out and even
Help my oppressor, when his own rejected him.
I have prayed for his soul.
I have prayed for his enlightening.
I have seen him when he was down.
I have caught him when he was most vulnerable.
Yes, I have refrained through divine compassion
to save him.
I know all his weak spots. I have helped to
shield him.
I am a proud, strong man, from a proud
strong race that
Has come to understand that your desire
to destroy my beauty
Is merely to cover up your ugliness.
Your desire to destroy my strength is merely
to hide
Your weakness.
Your desire to weaken my will is merely
to mend yours broken.
Your desire to oppress me stems from
you ignorance of happiness.
For me it would be totally unfair to claim
all men of one race
are haters of other races, from different
places, having different faces.
It would however be fair to say, it's a
disgrace, when the haters of
another race are allowed, by us, to live
in celebrated grace
as we often make them leaders of
the human races.

Placing them in elevated places.
It is then, that we, must fall in our
own graces, since we remain silent,
Making these destroyers of our human
races, place their own in
Our gracious places.
They pretend to justly represent, all the
hated oppressed faces.
Now you tell me, how can we have equity
amongst the different
Races, when we have racists in our
leadership places.
This could certainly lead to a horrifying
clash between the many
Beautiful, colorful faces of nature's
beautiful Races.

Chapter 48

I was suspended in a beautiful place.
I was suspended in a beautiful time.
The world was safe.
The world was all mine.
It was fine.
It was fine regardless of the time I chose to dine.
The world was safe, my lifestyle was just fine.
All my hours were mine.
There was no matter divine, to keep me in line,
and boy was everything just right for mine.
My life was just fine.
Just fine, until one day my world was penetrated
by a stranger
From another place, from another time.
No longer was my life simple,
No longer was my life carefree.
No longer was my life, my kind of fine.
For the very first time in life, I was
measured by another man's time.
For the very first time, a man forcefully
lived off my dime.
And for the first time I became aware,

Aware of motion,
Aware of Time.
My fear was new,
My fear was real.
The stranger reached in, suddenly,
Suddenly I found myself being ripped
with furious
Violence from my warm, lush, safe world
into his.
My fear was real.
My fear in this strange world with its strange
New faces, its new places, became my reality.
No longer did I have a world I could call
my own.
No longer was my world safe.
No longer was my world fine.
No longer was this world just mine.

Chapter 49

I find tremendous strength and pride each time I
Look into this mirror.
Yes, This Ethiopian looking back stands proud.
I'm a symbol of strength.
I am a symbol of cunning survival.
I am a symbol of gleaming courage.
I am a symbol of resistance to Racism.
I am a symbol of disappointment for oppressors,
For in all his unthinkable attempts to hurt, to destroy,
To downplay, to wipeout, my race, he has failed.
I am stronger.
Yes, much stronger than ever, with each attempt, my
Resolve to resist his tortuous mental game, grows
Stronger.
His attempts to psychologically main, always fail.
With his every attempt to inflict physical pain, my
Resolve grows stronger, and I show a physical gain.
I have the strength of not one, but Billions.
Yes, each time I look in this mirror, I see the
beauty in my face.
I take pride in my woman's grace.

Give it up,
Never will I, you, we, be eliminated from
this cruel human race.

Chapter 50

I would like to thing as time moves on,
so does the attitude of man.
If this is true, why does it seem my history
has remained the same?
Like life in a frying pan, and as time goes on
and on, the flames grow
Intensely stronger that strong.
Do we have any compassion for the abused man?
Seem like this abuse has been going on since
time began.
The hating of the colored man.
Shouldn't we be one?
Instead, I'm being forced in a corner,
making it harder and harder,
I thought my silent resolve, my silent tolerance,
Would help you to see the cruelty of your plan,
But all you seem to do is, whisper, whisper.
Spreading, just continuously spreading,
silent hate, for me, the Blackman.
This you have done from century, to century.
All I now seem to hear is your laughter,
never a sob, never a tear,
Not even one remorseful tear, for my
legitimate fear.
This has been going on for years!
Isn't it time you took my colored black hand?
Isn't it time you joined me? Yes, YOU
Mr. Whiteman!
Let's take a stand, as one, walking
hand in hand, with one peaceful Plan.
Let's take a stand against, against
human brutality, both against man and
God's land.
Let's take a united stand against,
a long standing brutal plan,
Designed against the none Whiteman.

Let's teach your children that Black
and white must walk hand in hand
As One.

Chapter 51

Birds and bees move freely through the trees.
Not being affected by any cold freeze.
Clothes were a bore, until something foreign
entered my door,
My life.
Now there is the razzle and dazzle, deliberately
Calculated by keeping score of man's
grand fashioned,
glamor stand, as never before in God's Plan.
It is only trite, that competition will lead to,
many, many
Long hard fighting, frightening sites.
It disturbed the harmony of the secluded night.
Disturbed the warmth of my tropical life.

Chapter 52

Sails soared high above the waves,
carrying many
Souls, that were brave.
Many openly welcomed Europe,
ignorant of their ways,
Until the Brave, smelled their fast

approaching graves!
Many sought refuge in Caves, far,
far, away,
even under the ocean waves.
Some hid low, where trees fail to grow.
There were many deaths.
Too many stories to be told.
So many stories that remain about those sold.
Yet the world grows Old,

Carrying loudly, many, many, groaning souls.
Waiting for sound, justice, to be found! Isn't this
An unselfishly, simple wish?

Chapter 53

The distant screams of happy children
takes me back
To distant thoughts, buried so far, they chill my
Feverish mind, and swell by breasts with the lust
for innocent uncaring happiness,
Of long unconcerned thoughts,
Of long unconcerned walks, through
bright green secluded
Pastures, disturbed only by the launching flops,
Flops of the blue, white headed shoe brown
morning birds
And the feathery whisper of the white winged doves,
Trying to escape my frightening human presence,
Climbing gracefully higher, and higher,
further and further,
Then dive, disappearing from sight on the
horizon of Gigantic cedar forests and tree.
They disappeared from sight, but lingered
in my mind,
As do the beautiful dense, dark magnificent
jungle,
An inviting welcomed refuge for me, we.
A jungle, providing Security far from
the whipping fields,
A forest Inviting, welcoming me,
as it keeps peering eyes
secure from the perils of Exposure,
discovery, then interruption, by
those who believe they have the right
to impose their ill will on
people free.
The sound of children's happy laughter,
though distant,
Drives me back, to a place of quiet

seclusion as I sit motionless
By the blue green algae pond, watching
for the illusive
Striped Red head, pond turtle.
Waiting for the moment when it's head
pops through the
Thick green blanket of algae for a
welcomed breath of
Cool tropical air, or watch the tall,
lanky brown and striped heron as it poises,
motionless, waiting for its unsuspecting
prey.
The sounds of children's screams and
happy laughter,
Brings me back to a time of happy innocence.
To a time of unchallenged adventure,
To a time when I streaked through lush forests,
To a time when I dashed across endless
grassy fields,
To a time when, naked and bare, I dived into
deep cool hidden river pools,
To a time when diving in secret bamboo
canopied pond and lakes
Was quenchingly Cool, WHERE we willingly
plaid the fool.
It takes me back to a time, when I lived,
When I had adventures, only kids, men,
boys and girls, find in fairy tales.
It takes me back to a time when the quiet seclusion,
Makes the missing of childhood so chillingly real.

Chapter 54

The power and roar of her steps are majestic,
It takes the searching soul to the spiritual bridge
Where ancestors, passed, but lost,
Lost in their quest to find that place which can only
Be quenching for the tired soul.
That Place many dreamed of, long, long, ago.
That place many still think of as they grow,

and continue to grow.
That final bride to take them home from
a place where
Un-resting souls still Roam.
That bride , when crossed, providing
refuge from the weight,
 And From the guilt of injustice, seeking
refuge from centuries,
Of injustice from the hands of the unjust.
Centuries of BRUTAL ABUSE,
Of one peoples force over another,
All for the gain of the other.

A bride providing refuge from, the
intense pain, the Pain so many
Had to endure.
This suffering still persist, making
these selfish acts most devilish.
Fuel by the fetish of homage to the
God called profit, this devilish
plan, these acts, Still persist.
Others forced in, to worship,
this evil, devilish God, we call profit.

Her dark deep pools remind me of
the hidden refuge found
Only in the dense wet jungle and
the damp cold
Caves of her misty blue mountains,
and in her deep
Distant green hills,
Where then, civilized men, taken
through uncivilized acts,
Sought the ultimate, freedom.
Her cool rocks, rough in texture,
but tough in character,
Draws images of these men.
Men, dark, cool, but made tough,
Tough by the roughness of the struggle.
The reality of their existence.
Man, made totally untrusting.
Man, made absolutely unrevealing.

Man' seeking refuge,
Through the warm blankets of the
dense dark tropical jungle,
as they protectively hug her mighty
curved shores.
Totally 'camouflages",
Hidden from total view.
Her towering thundering falls,
Her majestic mists, unwittingly offering
shelter from
The unrelenting hunters of the souls of man,
She is A bride, indeed, linking God's place.
A PLACE FOR THE TIRED SOUL.
Where?
Yes, this bridge, crosses beautiful Wyess falls!

Chapter 55

It was so real.
I could feel the thumps of my heart as I hustled
the lonely
Way home.
I don't remember where I went wrong,
Or even how I went wrong.
I just knew, that when I looked up, I was on a
high mountain,
SO high my spirits leaped, from my body,
I watched a rock
Fall into foreverness.
Falling into the blue black lagoon that
stretched into abbess of eternity.

I do not lie.

When rock made good its way home,
I finally knew how and what it means
to be that small, invisible dot, whispering
in the wind,
but never seen, never heard.
For that momentary moment, I finally

knew, I mean,
Really, really, knew absolute fear.
I could feel the thump of my very soul,
As something,
No ,No, not something,
Someone,
When someone, reached, grabbing me,
raising me, pulling,
Up, Up, higher and higher,
as the muddy cliff beneath my
feet began to subside.
It was a rapid slide.
Crashing with frightening might.
In marked contrast,
My savior gently rested me on solid
ground.
I still can't figure how I got there,
Or how I got here.
But I again found myself on my path home.
It wasn't a dream. I could still feel where
she grabbed me.
I could still see the imprints of her hand
where she held me.
She held me so I could see.

There was something she wanted me to be.
There was something she wanted me to do.
For that moment,
I knew my God was real.
I know she was always there for me.
My God had walked with me,
Or rather,
I had walked in the hands of the Creator.

Chapter 56

Day creeped upon night.
Causing widespread fright.
Claiming to give exceeding light, it fooled many,
they moved
White away from night.

For Light gave tremendous fight, causing
many to bash brains, as the
Light forced night to fight.
Robbing night of many, that found themselves
on any boat that
seem afloat, belonging to light.
Bounded like goats,
Stack on racks, with sores deep to their
bones, spreading from,
Whip scarred backs.
With light out of sight, many gave up the fight,
Giving way to a gruesome site,
Bodies develop gripe,
misguided fathers made desperate moves,
dives, suicide the prize,
When ship rolled,
For profits sold, many fight to avoid.
Captured to enriching government toll,
They-ed rather avoid presses Polls.
Light's spoils, caused great loss in
human life creating mass strife.

Chapter 57

It was dark,
There was darkness, then was made light,
Still darkness lived,
Then came light,
Out of the darkness came light.
Light that grew quickly, manufacturing fright,
Making the light move from night.
Far into places, out of sight of night.
Light could not exist, without night,
Light lost in light, with no night.
Light returned to night,
Not with love for night,
But with chattel to take, Money to make and
profits to Break,
Light unplugged a bloody fight.
Many nights engaged in gruesome fights.
Trying to make blackness, white.

Trying to change night to light,
Trying to make a black land white.
A totally ignorant and futile fight,
A victory totally out of sight.
Obviously light cannot be right.

Chapter 58

Maimed,

Drained, maimed and drained,
Both causing widespread pain.
Driving many insane.
Others use cocaine, blowing their brains,
Landing them into stifling drains.
Maimed by a change so mundane,
it effected cultural drain.
Cultural drain causing widespread social
change
And unyielding PAIN.

Chapter 59

Seen as goons,

We were used and abused.
A terrifying situation, soon become a permanent
Manifestation.
Manifestation causing human frustration and
Rapid forced migration, far from our OWN
land of creation.

Chapter 60

What drives man to create harrowing plans?
Is it greed?
Greed for a measly feed in vain materialistic THINGS?
What drives man to create terrifying plans that
Places humanity in a hateful hot pan?

What drives man to create dreaded plans,
 subjecting humanity to the day when
our meals will be as the disappearing
white sand.
What drives man to create plans spreading
Lustful Fear from year to year, with no
love to spear, Even for gentle dears?
How queer. Forcing the world to
remain unaware,
What drives man to create terrifying
plans for humanity
in his atomic bombs.
A thought subjectively fought out of
fear for the year when
All our plans, will become like the
motionless sand.
Isn't that a fascinating plans?

Chapter 61

Native land big and wide,
Often the objective of genocide.
Being robbed of many a child, under the guise
That they are wild.
They are uncivilized.
Creating a plan that still remain because only
Few sympathize,
Even with soul wrenching cries from the
sad wise child,
To the so called civilized.

Chapter 62

There is a cling, there is a clang
In a land oppressed by the sins of one man,
towards plural man.
Men in chains, their burdens manifestly grave,
Forcing the brave to become slaves to
Those greedily insane.
There is a cling, there is a clang,

Chains hang around the bleeding hands of a
Suppressed man.
Is there a genuinely conscious plan to free
this compressed land?
There is cling,
There is clang,
There exist a harrowing plan, for
The native man working, in this hot, hot homeland.

Chapter 63

Mystically blue, mystically deep,
Mystically wide, it remains like a child.
Wide in places hot, wide in places cold,
Never, ever, growing old.
Now it's calm, then it's not.
Isn't this divinely mystical?

Chapter 64

Coined by hands moving as fast as they can,
Bringing to life, from clay found below the river sand,
An objective of one man's thought,
Of one man's soul,
Of one man's desire.
The turning, the molding, the final compounding,
Of time,
Of adventure,
Of pressure,
Of pain,
Released from hidden dreams of things yet unseen,
Of things only perceived, of things that gleam.
Gleaming from one man's soul.
Only with limited understanding,
Only with limited thought.
Coined by hands moving as far as they can to trap,
The minutes, the microseconds of divine revelation.
Trying to trap the wisdom,
The awe,
The total reflection of an image only found in mans

Soul, making it solid, in form, in color, in presence,
when complete,
As completely close to the revelation as one can get,
It is solidified with the heart of the passionate.
The fire that only artists, philosophers and
children have.
It is likened to the burning drive to discover
the plan upon which
The good in our souls directs us.
Where perfection, in perfection, is easily had.
Where we understand what it means to "drink milk,
And eat honey".
Where we dream of the reality to return
to virgin innocence.
The reality of my soul,
That will be where we dream, long after,
my body is gone.
Long after generations have passed.
That will stand steadfast while man's
laws change time after time.
I look,
I see,
Yes, I see my soul trapped, in a little brown vase.

Chapter 65

My mind wonders to silent distant places,
yet undiscovered.
Every time I lay quickly, motionless, barely breathing,
feeling every thump of my arteries. As I stare
at the wondrous
beauty of the little stares, so distant it seem to,
beacons the deepest reaches of one's soul.
A place where good spirits soar.
It beacons,
Come,
Come, don't resist,
Give in,
With its beauty, untamed it reached out for
those built the same.
As it silently winks back,
the dawn reaches
From the sky, telling you,
It's ok,
I'll be Back, here, when you return, it's ok,
your safe.

The mystery and magic of time and
space boggling the beautiful mind,
It Brings my lonely troubled soul, close within.
As close to the universe as one could ever be.
So close to creation itself, I can look back and see
The limp motionless me.
The reality of the thought chills the mind, the body,
The thirsty soul.
Thought of power of the almighty himself,
Rushes back with a vengeance,
Making the meek, tiny me, only more a reality.
The loneliness becomes stifling, forcing the soul to
Seek shelter from the uncountable tiny eyes,
as they flash back.
Then and only then, I know, I'm not alone.
God in his wisdom and glory, must have made

more like me,
Like me, somewhere out there!
Praying, Like me,
For someone, like me.

www.ingramcontent.com/pod-product-compliance
Lightning Source LLC
Chambersburg PA
CBHW072209090426
42740CB00012B/2457